Tintin and Snowy

Life is never boring for this intrepid reporter and his faithful dog.
Each day brings a new adventure!

Thomson and Thompson

The dimwitted detectives are immediately fooled
by the mysterious museum thief.

- HERG
★

THE ADVENTURE⌐ ⌐⌐ ⌐⌐⌐⌐⌐

THE E

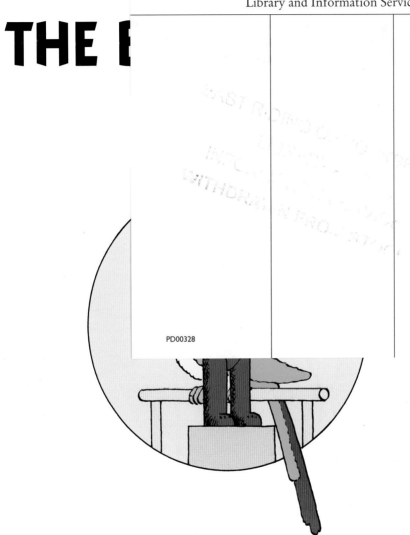

EGMONT

Original Album: *The Broken Ear*
Renewed Art Copyright © 1946, 1974 by Casterman, Belgium
Text Copyright © 1975 by Egmont UK Limited

Translated by Leslie Lonsdale-Cooper and Michael Turner

Additional Material
Art Copyright © Hergé/Moulinsart 2013
Text Copyright © Moulinsart 2013

www.casterman.com
www.tintin.com

This edition published in 2013 by Egmont UK Ltd.
The Yellow Building,
1 Nicholas Road, London W11 4AN

egmont.co.uk

1 3 5 7 9 10 8 6 4 2
ISBN: 978 1 4052 6699 4

55030/1

General Alcazar

Forever battling his rival for control of San Theodoros,
in his spare time General Alcazar likes to play practical jokes
with explosive punch lines!

Alonso and Ramón

Ruthless villain Ramón and his partner in crime Alonso
are determined to beat Tintin in the hunt for the stolen statue.

Corporal Diaz

Allegiances are always shifting in San Theodoros. Demoted from his position as colonel, Corporal Diaz is determined to get his revenge.

Pablo

Originally sent to harm Tintin, Pablo ends up saving the reporter's life!
Another character who is quick to change sides, but this time for the good!

Ridgewell

Long-lost explorer Ridgewell has traded the big city for life in the jungle.

PAINTED
POSTS
DAHOMEY

BAPENDE
MASK

15

HEAD OF
CARVED
WOOD
PACHACAMAO

116

No. 3542
ARUMBAYA FETISH
The Arumbaya tribe
live along the banks
of the River Coliflor
in the Republic of
San Theodoros,
South America

Closing
time!

Goodness! It's
five o'clock
already...

RRRRING

Come on, lazy-bones!
Time to get up!

Toreador, on guard now!
Toreador! ♪ Toreador!
Toreador! ♪♪

Toreador... ♫♪ tra la la
la la... ♫ Toreador...
Fond eyes gaze and
adore... ♫♪ ♫

PLURIARC
BURMA

?!¿
? !

Knees bent, arms full stretch!
Ready... up... and down
... and up... and down...

Now for a bath; that's the way
to wake up in the morning.

Here is the eight
o'clock news...

Details are just coming
in of a robbery at the
Museum of Ethnography.
A rare fetish - a sacred
tribal object - disappeared
during the night...

① 1

The loss was discovered this morning by a museum attendant. It is believed the thief must have hidden in the gallery overnight and slipped out when the staff arrived for work. No evidence of a break-in has been found . . .

Come on Snowy! To the Museum of Ethnography!

The Director? I'm afraid he's engaged: the police are here . . .

Now, to recapitulate . . . You say the attendant locked the doors last night at 17.12 hours; he noticed nothing unusual. He came on duty this morning at seven. At 07.14 he observed that exhibit No. 3542 was missing and immediately raised the alarm. Right? . . . Now this attendant: is he reliable?

Absolutely! Above suspicion! He's been with us for over twelve years and never given the least cause for complaint.

Besides, the fetish has no intrinsic value. In my judgement, it would only be of interest to a collector . . .

Great snakes! The Thompsons!

Why, it's our friend Tintin!

Have you any leads?

Well, the Arumbaya fetish has no in . . . er . . . no instinctive value . . . The solution is quite simple: it was removed by a collector.

To be precise: it was collect-ed by a remover.

Some hours later . . .

This is the book. I'm sure it has something about the Arumbayas.

A.J. WALKER

TRAVELS IN THE AMERICAS

LONDON 1875

Aha! This is interesting . . . Listen, Snowy. "Today we met our first Arumbayas. Long, black, oily hair framed their coffee-coloured faces. They were armed with long blow-pipes which they employ to shoot darts poisoned with curare . . ." You hear that, . . . Snowy?

We decided to stay there. The sun generosity and gave us a plentiful

ARUMBAYA armed with a blow-pipe

. . . Curare! . . . the terrible vegetable poison which paralyses one's breathing! . . . Oh! "Arumbaya fetish" . . . But . . . but . . . it's the very one that's been stolen!

I therefore made an accurate sketch they urged me to go

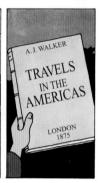

ARUMBAYA FETISH

we were very well treated. Later we

Odd coincidence, don't you think, Snowy? . . . Snowy isn't interested . . . he's gone to sleep . . . I think I'll follow suit.

The next morning . . .

Help! It's bewitched!

Hello! . . . Hello? . . . Hello!? . . . Is that you, sir?

Yes, who is that? . . . Oh, it's you, Fred . . . What? The fetish? My goodness me! I'll come at once . . .

Half an hour later . . .

Excuse me . . . Is this the house where Mr Balthazar lived?

Yes, this is it. Ooh, sir, what a tragedy! . . . Such a polite gentleman! . . . And all that learning! . . . Maybe he wasn't all that regular with the rent, but he always paid it in the end. And such a way with animals! A parrot and three white mice, that's what he had . . .

I . . .

I'm minding the parrot for the time being. But I can't keep it. So if you know of anyone . . .

Of course . . . I was wondering if I might look at Mr Balthazar's room?

I'll take you up. Such a character he was . . . sniff . . . I can still see him . . . his everlasting black velvet suit, and that big hat . . . And all that smoking! A pipe in his mouth all day long, he had. But he never touched the drink . . .

Oh?

Here is his room . . .

This is where we found him . . . sniff . . . They had to send for a locksmith . . . the door was locked from the inside . . . The gas was whistling out of the ring.

A little scrap of grey flannel . . .

And so clever he was . . . Just look at those flowers: you can almost smell them . . .

You knew Mr Balthazar well?

Er . . . that's to say . . . not intimately . . .

If by any chance you found a parrot-lover! . . . It's such a friendly bird!

Naturally, I'll remember you. Goodbye and thanks.

An accident? . . . Funny sort of accident, I'd say . . .

A very funny accident! . . . The gas was whistling out of the ring. So, if the tap was on when Balthazar went to bed he'd have heard it. Unless he was drunk; but he never touched drink. Therefore someone turned the tap on after the sculptor was dead, since the gas wasn't strong enough to kill the parrot. And that someone was wearing something made of grey flannel and smoking a cigarette . . .

. . . witness the piece of cloth and the cigarette end, which couldn't have belonged to the victim: he only smoked a pipe, and he wore a velvet suit. So Mr Balthazar was murdered. He was murdered because he'd probably made a replica of the Arumbaya fetish for someone. And someone didn't want him to talk . . . Someone? . . . Someone? . . . Who-can that 'someone' be? . . . How can I find out?

Great snakes! . . . Why not?!

④

Excuse me, but I've been thinking. I'll buy Mr Balthazar's parrot.

The parrot? Ooooh, sir!

If you'd only been two minutes sooner! I just sold it. The gentleman who bought it was here a moment ago; you must have passed him.

Just my luck!

Look, there he goes! You see the gentleman with a parcel under his arm? That's him.

Let's hope he'll agree to resell it to me.

Grrreat greedy-guts!

Hey, you! . . . D'you always behave like that? Let me tell you, I'm not used to being insulted!

Perdone, Señor.

Very well! But another time you'll be in trouble!

But . . . I assure the señor . . .

GRRREAT GREEDY-GUTS!

Oh, help! It's a regular punch-up . . . Ooh! The parrot! The parrot!!

The parrot!!!

GRRREAT GREEDY-GUTS!

Estúpido! Imbécil! Great greedy-guts! Look what you do: my beautiful parrot ees escapado! Ees perdido!

The only witness to Balthazar's death, the only one who could have talked, and there he goes.

The parrot ees give me by my grandfather. Ay, qué desastre . . . All same, muchas gracias for try to catch heem.

That's quite all right.

"Give to me by my grandfather". Why tell a lie? I wonder, could he be interested in the parrot for the same reason as me?

Meanwhile...

It's raining, Professor. Don't forget your umbrella ... and remember your glasses.

Don't worry, Ernestine. My glasses are in the pocket of my jacket ... and I'll take my umbrella.

PWARK

PWARK
PWARK ?

What a curious-looking creature!

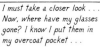

I must take a closer look ... Now, where have my glasses gone? I know I put them in my overcoat pocket ...

Oh, it's a bird.

Good morning. How d'you do? Pleased to meet you!

I ... er ... do forgive me, sir. I'm so absent-minded ... Would you believe it: I mistook you for a bird!

Your advertisement reads "Lost: magnificent parrot. Large reward. Finder contact 26 Labrador Road." It will be in tonight's paper, sir.

Ees necesario to make advertisement about the parrot.

There: "Lost: magnificent parrot ..." Look, there are two notices, I'll try the first address: it's nearer than the other.

The sooner the better!

Grrreat greedy-guts!

RRRRING

I came about the parrot. Are you the gentleman who ... ?

Ah, yes! Do come in!

Let's have a look ...

It's him all right! I can't thank you enough. You wouldn't believe what he means to me. Please take the reward.

Goodbye, and thank you.

It's me who's grateful!

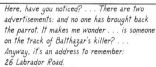

Ah, it's you!
Caramba! Ees the young man who try to catch the parrot!

Come on! Start talking! You wanted the parrot?
Si! Thees bird he ees mine. You steal heem. I make complain to the policía!

Really? Go right ahead. There's the 'phone; ring the police . . .

Now, let's be serious. I want to know why you're interested in our feathered friend . . .

I'm waiting . . .

? ?

WHEEE THWACK ZZINNG ?** BANG

I saw you were trapped, so I came up quietly and switched off the light.
I have time to throw puñal at heem.

A few inches to the left and . . . pfff! Curtains for Tintin! I'll have to watch out; they'll stick at nothing!

I hear the puñal, he go whack into chair. I only miss heem by thees much . . .
I know, I know . . . you need more practice.

That night, at 21 London Road . . .

BING CRACK CRR

CLACK
That Mr and Mrs Dove! They've quarrelled once too often!

Have you quite finished up there?!

SHUT UP! I AM BALTHAZAR!

HELP! HELP!

Ooh, Colonel! It's the ghost of Mr Balthazar! I heard his voice! It's him! I know it!
Ghosts? Rubbish! Stuff and nonsense! . . . We'll see . . . By the left, quick march!

Close ranks! . . . Load arms! . . . Fix bayonets!

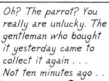

Road hog! He couldn't have been closer if he'd tried to run you down!

Yes, he deliberately swerved to the left!

Are you hurt?

No, thanks, I had time to jump clear. I wouldn't have fallen if I hadn't tripped over the edge of the pavement.

I managed to get his number ... Wait ... 169 ... Yes, 169 MW ... That's it. 169 MW ... You'll have to ask the police ...

169 MW. Thank you!

... I tell you, if that idiot hadn't warned him I'd have settled his hash!

Si, si, but truth ees you meess heem and from now he ees on hees guard. Ciertamente, knife ees better!

In that case, you'll have to practise harder: you always throw too far to the right ...

Only a leetle ...

That's it ... 169 MW ... Doctor Eugene Trebblebob, 120 Minstrel's Way ... Good!

This time I'm sure I'm on the right track.

MINSTREL'S WAY

Here we are.

?

169 MW

Wrong number! ... That man who told me can't have seen it clearly ...

Anyway, it's possible they used false number plates on their car ... Oh! ...

!

EUREKA!

?

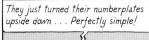

Ramón, if you lay a finger on that parrot you're a dead duck!

YEOW!

Mala bestia! Kill heem!

Carrramba! . . . Missed again! . . .

? ?

Rodrigo Tortilla, you've killed me!

Rodrigo Tortilla!

So it was Tortilla!

Lying crook! . . . Pretending to be a doctor on a study trip to Europe . . . But all he wanted was to steal the fetish . . . and the swine succeeded. By getting rid of Balthazar, he thought he'd covered his tracks. But he reckoned without our feathered friend! . . . I've got his address. I'm going to fix a meeting. He won't suspect anything . . .

Hello? . . . Is that the Hotel Liberty? . . . May I speak to Mr Tortilla, please . . .

Mr Tortilla? . . . I'm so sorry, but he's gone, sir . . . Yes, to South America . . . Yes, he went to Le Havre, he sailed at midday . . . The boat? . . . It was called "Ville de Lyon" . . .

That tells me all I need to know . . .

We're beaten! . . . There goes Tortilla peacefully sailing away to South America . . . If only that brainless parrot had talked just one day sooner . . .

. . . next bulletin at eleven o'clock . . . Now here is some late shipping news . . .

Do we have to keep listening to that wretched radio?

The strike of dockworkers at the French port of Le Havre has spread today. More than a dozen ships are now delayed. Among vessels not expected to sail before midnight tomorrow is the "Ville de Lyon", bound for South America . . .

Caramba! All is not lost, Ramón: we have time to get there!

Now, clever Señor Tortilla, the fun begins!

Several days later . . .

Well? Still nothing?

Nothing. No sign of heem anywhere!

Perhaps he see us and he keep to hees cabin . . . Or maybe he nevaire come aboard thees ship . . . Een thees case . . .

Ssh! Someone's coming . . .

Did you see? . . .

That feegure . . . eet could be . . .

Tintin, couldn't it?

No, ciertamente ees impossible! . . . Also, how could he know?

Sssh!

Or him?

It's crazy! We've started seeing Tintins around every corner! They're all fairly short . . . OK . . . But what does that prove?

. . . Ees right.

But no, ees not right! Eet ees heem! Ees first one, thees one in the cap. I remember heem: ees in same aeroplane and he seet behind us. Ees following us. I tell you, ees Tintin!

All right, there's only one answer. He's got to go!

Esta noche . . . tonight, after the dinner, we feex heem good!

That evening . . .

Now don't forget: aim a little more to the left . . .

Goodnight! . . . Oh!

Goodnight to you!

A weeg! Ees wearing a weeg! Ciertamente ees heem!

Careful, he's coming! Now above all, don't miss!

OOH! . . . HELP! . . . MURDER! HELP!

STOP THEM!

HELP! HELP! MURDER!

Madre! Ees close theeng . . . And to think I meess heem as well! . . . Ees your fault. You weeth your "Leetle more to the left"!

Well, it's the first time you landed where you aimed . . . Anyway, it's probably a good thing you didn't hit him, since it wasn't Tintin!

Ees right. But I could swear eet ees heem . . . Only hees voice when he shout ees not heem.

There's still the other: the little old man.

Next morning . . .

You are ready? We now go to work weeth thees leettle old man . . .

Ees heem!! He spy on us!

OK, let's see. We'll follow him . . .

No, not that way. We aren't sure it's him. I've a better idea: come with me . . .

Get it? If it's Tintin, he must be wearing a false beard. So . . .

ZZZ
ZZZZ
ZZZ
ZZ

Steady! . . . You're nearly there . . . A little to the right . . . Gently . . . Back a bit . . . That's it! . . . Now!

14

No, it isn't Tintin!

Now we're sure Tintin isn't aboard we can really get down to finding Tortilla . . .

. . . weeth fetish!

Ah, there's our steward . . . Will you join us for a drink?

Thanks . . . I see you're up bright and early. Not like some I could mention . . . Take your fellow countryman in cabin 17 . . . Never shows his nose outside the door . . .

Why not? Sick?

He says he is, but I don't believe a word of it. Anyway, he hasn't left his cabin since we sailed . . . Has all his meals there . . . Well, cheers!

Cheers!

You heard that? The passenger in 17 . . .

And you'll never believe it . . . Just between the three of us . . . the passenger . . . isn't a man, isn't a woman . . . but . . . an omelette!

? ? ?

Ha! ha! ha! Now wait for it . . . D'you know why? . . . Because he's called Tortilla, and in Spanish tortilla means . . .

. . . an omelette! Ha! ha! ha! That's rich!

Ees beeg joke! . . .

Got to go now . . . If the Captain sees me here I'll catch it . . . And you wouldn't want to drop me in the drink, eh?

Get away with you . . . you're a real caution!

That was a good one . . . drop in the drink . . . Get it?

Thanks to that nitwit we've found Tortilla . . . Ramón, the fetish is ours!

At last!

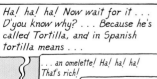

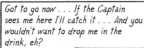

⑮

That night . . .

SPLASH

Next morning the ship arrives off Los Dopicos, capital of the Republic of San Theodoros, South America

Have you heard? . . . That Tortilla . . . He's disappeared! He must have been pushed overboard! There'd been a struggle in his cabin!

How shocking! . . . Do they know who did it?

They do indeed, gentlemen! . . . Come on now! . . . Get your hands up . . . fast!

Caramba! It's Tintin! I might have known!

Keep a close watch on them till the police arrive . . .

I am Colonel Jimenez, regular army.

Captain Maldemer . . . I have two prisoners I'd like to hand over, Colonel.

These two? . . . I know them both . . . dangerous crooks, wanted by our police.

Good idea of yours to meet the boat . . . Excellent . . . But there's still the fetish . . .

Don't worry . . . they won't have it for long!

. . . And that's the whole story. Look, here's the fetish they stole from the wretched Tortilla. Does anything in particular strike you about it?

I reckon it's another fake. The right ear isn't broken.

Exactly. So we still need to know two things. First, where's the real fetish . . . and then, what are all these gangsters really after?

RAT TAT TAT

Come in!

A letter for Mr Tintin, sir. A police launch just brought it.

Republic of San Theodoros
Ministry of Justice
Los Dopicos

The Minister presents his compliments to Mr Tintin and requests his presence ashore to assist in the interrogation of two suspects. Mr Tintin is further invited to bring with him the stolen fetish. An officer will meet Mr Tintin on shore and put himself at his disposal.

Things are beginning to move. I'll just get myself ready and then I'll go.

See you later! Good luck!

Thanks. Goodbye.

Don't forget, we'll be sailing tonight at eight o'clock.

Don't worry, I'll be back. I don't want to get stuck in this place!

All right then, that's understood. You'll pick me up here at 19.00 hours.

Yes, sir.

Now we just have to wait for that obliging officer to come and put himself at my disposal!

Hey! My suitcase!

Ah! . . . It's still there . . . Whew!

What a fright!

That's him, isn't it?

Yes, he's the one!

Will you come with us, señor? . . .

Ah, there you are. Excellent.

Why all the soldiers everywhere?

There's talk of a revolution . . .

CUARTEL DE SAN JUAN V

tell m you will find in harbour. He has with him a small white dog. If you don't believe this letter, open his case . . . xxx

RAT TAT TAT

Come in!

This is the man, Captain.

Good. Open your case!

Captain, I don't know whether you're fully in the picture . . . I was sent for by the Minister of Justice to help in the interrogation of the two . . .

Cut out the talk! Do as you're told! I said open your case!

Very well, Captain . . . but I warn you, I shall complain of your behaviour . . .

Bombs! My informant was right: he's a terrorist!

Hold him! Take him to the cell block at once . . . to await the firing squad!

Captain, it's all a trick, I tell you! My case was stolen, and switched with this one!

OK, OK, we know all that! To the cells!

Well, well, here I am again . . . in the soup!

Still, it's not so bad. The launch from the "Ville de Lyon" is due to pick me up at seven. When I don't appear they'll go back to the ship and alert the Captain . . . He'll get me out easily enough.

Doesn't that dog belong to the lad they just took in?

Yes, and I guess he'll have a long wait for his master . . .

19.00 hours . . .

Perdone, señor teniente, but are you waiting for a young man to take out to the "Ville de Lyon"?

Yes, how d'you know that?

Because he said to tell you not to wait for him. And here's a letter he asked me to give you . . .

"To the Captain of the Ville de Lyon." All right, thank you.

That's that taken care of!

There's the launch going back. They'll warn the Captain.

. . . And there's the letter the man gave me.

Las Dopicos

Dear Captain,
    As you know, I planned to continue my trip with you.
    However, something new has come up concerning the theft of the fetish, forcing me to stay longer in Las Dopicos.
    I am extremely sorry if I have incon-

What's happening? It must be nearly eight o'clock and the launch still isn't back . . .

TOOOOT TOOOT

That's the "Ville de Lyon"!

They're weighing anchor . . . sailing without me!!

This time it's hopeless . . . I can't see any way to get myself off the hook . . .

And next morning . . .

Squad! . . . Ready! . . .

Take aim . . .

Stop! Don't shoot!

Hello? What's up? Have I been reprieved?

Comrades! The revolution has triumphed! General Tapioca has fled, the tyrant is on the run! Our glorious General Alcazar is now in command!

Long live General Alcazar!

Down with Tapioca!

¡Fuera los tiranos!

¡Viva la libertad!

In which case, sir, you are free . . .

That suits me!

Colonel! . . . Ah, Colonel! At last I've found you!

Now what's going on?

What is it Colonel? Have they caught General Tapioca?

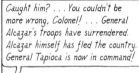

Caught him? . . . You couldn't be more wrong, Colonel! . . . General Alcazar's troops have surrendered. Alcazar himself has fled the country. General Tapioca is now in command!

Are you sure, Colonel?

Sure as eggs are eggs. I've been looking for you for half an hour to break the news!

Hmm . . . . In that case . . .

Comrades! The rebellion is crushed! General Alcazar has fled, the tyrant is on the run! Let us all swear allegiance to our glorious General Tapioca!

Long live General Tapioca!

Down with Alcazar!

¡Fuera los tiranos!

¡Viva la libertad!

I'm terribly sorry, sir, but the way things are, I'll have to carry out my orders and shoot you.

Take aim . . .

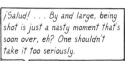

¡Viva el héroe!

Hooray!

Golly! . . . Look, there's Tintin!

Go and see what's happening, Colonel . . . and bring that young man here to me. I want to meet him.

I've already been shot three times . . . so a fourth time makes no odds to me. I'm used to it.

Here he is, General . . . he was sentenced to death by General Tapioca. Our men arrived just as the firing squad were going to shoot him. They had their rifles up, and this courageous fellow was still shouting "Long live General Alcazar!"

¡Muy bien! I am General Alcazar, and I need men like you! As a mark of my appreciation, I appoint you colonel aide-de-camp.

Thanks very much . . . but I'd like my hand back!

But . . . don't you think, General, it might be wiser to make him a corporal? We only have forty-nine corporals, whereas there are already three thousand four hundred and eighty-seven colonels. So . . .

Enough!!

I shall do as I like! I'm in command! But since you consider we are short of corporals I will add to their number. Colonel Diaz, I appoint you corporal!

Yes, General!

Here's your colonel's commission, young man. Now, go and get yourself kitted out. Corporal Diaz here will take you to the tailor.

Jolly old tailor!

A colonel's uniform for our young friend? . . . Excellent! I had this all ready for Colonel Fernandez, who fled with General Tapioca . . . He was just the same size . . . And for yourself? . . . A corporal's outfit? I have just the thing . . .

My career is in ruins. But I'll have my revenge, on you and that confounded General Alcazar!

That night . . . Comrades, we have a new member . . . an officer who preferred to resign his commission rather than continue to serve a tyrant! He will take the oath.

I swear obedience to the laws of our society. I promise to fight against tyranny with all my strength. My watchword henceforward is the same as yours: liberty or death!

The next morning . . .

Where's my new aide-de-camp? Not here yet?

Not yet, General.

As soon as he arrives send him in. We have work to do . . .

Very good, sir. At once.

Colonel! . . . How on earth did I come to be a colonel? I don't remember a thing . . .

However, I'm still looking for the fetish, and to do that I must resign my commission.

No, gentlemen: impossible. The General is waiting for his ADC. He won't see anyone this morning.

Them!

Heem!

Oh!

Ah, there you are, Colonel. We must get down to work. As for you, gentlemen: I cannot receive you this morning . . . Come, Colonel!

No more need for me to resign, for the time being.

The General choose heem!

It's crazy!

Thees ees bad!

Yes, now we'll have to deal with him all over again!

Meanwhile . . .

His office window is open . . . So far so good!

It's a delicate position . . .

Yes, very delicate.

I'm sorry, Your Excellency, but the General can't see you this morning. The General is extremely busy . . .

Checkmate, my dear Colonel!

Goodness! You're right!

23

BING

BING

? * ⌐ * *

My dear Colonel, I shall never forget how you saved my life!

No, General, let's say I managed to save both our lives . . .

Caramba! Back to square one again!

We've been taken for a ride. The fetish he had in his suitcase was a fake. But he certainly knows where the real one is. So tonight, we'll have him picked up . . .

And we make heem tell us where the real fetish ees . . .

That evening . . .

What a wind! . . . We're in for a storm tonight . . .

Look! . . . He's coming!

HELP! HELP!

Whack! and off he goes to dreamland!

Get off!

An hour later . . .

That's agreed then: as soon as he's told us where the fetish is, we get rid of him for good!

Ees right: he gives us beeg trouble.

THUMP
THUMP
THUMP

Come!

We got him.

Good. Bring him in here . . .

Welcome to our humble abode, my dear Colonel! . . . Sit down and have a chat . . .

A neat trick, Colonel. The idea of putting a fake fetish in your suitcase wasn't bad . . . But now we'd like to know where the real one is . . .

Me too . . . I'd like to know that . . .

Come on! Cut the funny stuff! Where is it?

I've told you, I don't know.

Ah! Like that, is it? Very well.

I'll give you three minutes to answer my question. After that, a little squeeze with my finger and . . . click! . . . Understand?

BOMMM

BRROM

*

Caramba! Ees beeg storm! . . .

One minute . . .

If only . . . if only I could free myself . . .

Tintin? What's happened to Tintin?

Ees no use to struggle so hard, amigo. Ees good strong cord and tied very nice. You take my word for that . . .

Two minutes . . .

I must tell them something . . . doesn't matter what it is . . . otherwise I'm done for.

Thirty seconds to go . . .

All right. I'll tell you where to find the fetish . . .

Aha! . . . I knew we'd come to an understanding in the end. Where is it?

It . . . er . . . well, briefly, it's in my trunk aboard the "Ville de Lyon".

Thanks . . . That's all we wanted you to tell us.

And now we don't need you any more you can say your prayers! You're going to die!

Pronto, pronto, Alonso. You know I am upset by capital punishment . . .

Quick! He must have gone through the window! . . .

Down there! Ees trying to reach the road!

He cannot be far away . . .

There! Spot on! Every time a coconut!

Good old Snowy! There you are!

CÁRCEL

Good morning. I've brought you some customers!

Ten o'clock, and he still isn't here!

Now, quickly, back to the General.

RAT TAT TAT

Come in!

DYNAM

That's it . . . All I need is a light . . .

DYNA

DYN

DYNAM

¡Madre! I've forgotten my matches! . . .

DYNA

Hmm! . . . Surely I can smell something burning . . .

DYNA

Caramba! Back to square one again!

Check to your king, General!

Diablo! . . . I must watch what I'm doing . . .

! ?
That's checkmate, General!

¡Mil millón bombas! You dare to beat me, your General?!

BANG BANG
BANG
BANG BANG
BANG

Ha! ha! ha! ha!

It's a little joke I often play on my officers, to frighten them. Naturally, my gun's always loaded with blanks.

That reminds me of an aide I had a while back. Ha! ha! ha! ha! . . . One day, he beat me at chess. I pulled out my gun . . .

This time, General Alcazar, your reign is at an end! Liberty or death!

DYNA

I pulled out my gun and fired. Ha! ha! ha! ... Just imagine, the chap fainted ... Ha! ha! ha! ... And best of all, can you believe it, next day he had jaundice! ... Imagine! Jaundice!

DYNA

BOOM

AL GENERAL OLIVARO LIBERTADOR DE SAN TEODORO 1805-1899
Justice is done!

AL GENERAL OLIVARO LIBERTADOR DE SAN TEODORO 1805-1899

An attack!
The General's palace! ... It's over there!
Another revolution? ...

It's all right! Quite all right! General Alcazar is unharmed!

Idiot! Surely you know that if you just put dynamite against a wall it only produces a loud bang: you need to bury it ... Now, it's back to square one again!

Next morning ...
Hello? ... Is that General Alcazar's palace? ... Oh, it's you, doctor. How is the General? ... What? ... What?? ... JAUNDICE!!!

Jaundice, yes ... Caused by shock, you know ...

RAT TAT TAT
Come!

Who is it?

R.W. Trickler, representative, General American Oil. All right, show him in.

Good morning. Do please sit down.

Well, Colonel, the reason I'm here . . . I heard yesterday . . .

Please excuse me . . .

Yes, of course . . .

RRRING

Hello? . . . Hello? . . . Yes, Captain . . . What?! . . . They've escaped!

We are free, and soon the fetish ees ours!

And soon we'll have our revenge too; we have old scores to settle with Tintin!

Now, sir . . . I'm all yours . . .

Well, a geological survey party has just announced evidence of oil deposits in the Gran Chapo region . . . the desert lying partly in your own country and partly in the neighbouring territory, the Republic of Nuevo-Rico.

General American Oil seeks to obtain a concession to work these fields. Obviously, your government will have an interest in the profits that would accrue . . .

I see. I'm afraid General Alcazar is ill, and I cannot . . .

Of course, of course. But you could render us invaluable service. I mentioned that part of the oil fields lie in Nuevo-Rican territory. My company wishes to exploit the whole region: so it follows that you must take over the area.

But . . . that would mean war!

Unfortunately, yes. But what can one do? You can't make an omelette without breaking eggs, can you, Colonel?

So, here's the reason for my visit. We will give you 100,000 dollars in cash if you will persuade General Alcazar to undertake the campaign . . . Is it a deal?

You're making a big mistake in refusing my offer. But, just as you wish, Colonel! Goodbye!

A dangerous fellow! He could wreck all our plans. I must have a word with Rodriguez about him . . .

(31)

Yes, Rodriguez, I will offer 10,000 dollars to be rid of him . . .

If Your Excellency were so kind as to entrust the money to me I am sure matters could be arranged . . .

So, that's a deal, Pablo? 5,000 dollars for an accident to happen to Colonel Tintin . . .

OK. The accident will occur tonight!

Bravo, Ramón! Aim like that tonight and Tintin will be no more than an unpleasant memory!

Caramba! Missed again!

OOOOOOH!

Mercy, señor Colonel! Mercy! I will tell everything . . .

Ramón! What on earth . . . ? Are you hurt?

What happened? Quick, tell me . . .

Oooh! . . . He keell me! . . .

Here, sit down . . .

Ooooh!

YEOWW!

Who was it? Who paid you to get rid of me?

It was Rodriguez . . . Mr Trickler's right hand man . . .

I see . . . Now get up. I forgive you.

Oh, thank you, thank you, señor Colonel. I am your devoted servant . . . for life!

I really think he meant it, poor devil!

You shouldn't trust a rascal like that. You're far too gullible!

Some days later . . .

The General is back: he's completely recovered. At the moment he's talking to Mr Trickler.

Look, General . . . just think . . . It's wholly to your advantage. As I say, you declare war on Neuvo-Rico, and you annexe the oilfields. My company makes a profit on the oil and your country gets 35%. But naturally you deduct 10% for personal expenses . . .

Yes . . . very neat . . . I accept.

Excellent, General. I was sure we would understand one another.

By the way, General . . . that Colonel Tintin, in whom you seem to have so much confidence . . . Let me give you some advice: don't trust him. I won't say any more now . . .

Good morning, my dear Colonel . . . The General awaits you . . .

Good morning, General. I'm glad to see you're better. I . . .

What is it now?

!?! He doesn't seem in a very good mood today . . .

Send him in.

Basil Bazarov

KORRUPT ARMS GMBH

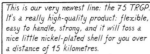
Good morning, General Alcazar. I happened to be passing through your country, and thought I'd show you our latest models.

This is our very newest line: the 75 TRGP. It's a really high-quality product: flexible, easy to handle, strong, and it will toss a nice little nickel-plated shell for you over a distance of 15 kilometres.

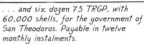
Oho! This could be serious. Listen, Ramón. Las Dopicos. A detachment of Nuevo-Rican soldiers crossed into the territory of San Theodoros and opened fire on a border post. Guards returned the fire and a violent battle ensued. The Nuevo-Ricans were forced to retire across the frontier, having sustained heavy losses. The only casualty on our side was a corporal, wounded by a cactus spine.

The airport . . .

Now we are off to San-Facion . . . the Nuevo-Rican capital.

Very good, sir.

. . . and six dozen 75 TRGP, with 60,000 shells, for the government of San Theodoros. Payable in twelve monthly instalments.

To General Mogador's palace.

Very good, señor.

Half an hour later . . .

Back to the airport.

Si, señor.

That's Señor Bazarov's private plane . . .

. . . and six dozen 75 TRGP, with 60,000 shells, for the government of Nuevo-Rico. Payment in twelve monthly instalments.

Here he comes, back already to Las Dopicos.

Well?

All done. Another fat order . . . and something to fix Colonel Tintin too!

Now pay attention. It's a time bomb, with a clock. It's set to explode at exactly eleven o'clock tomorrow morning . . . And you'd better succeed this time!

I'll succeed, chief! Liberty or death!

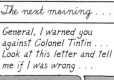
The next morning . . .

General, I warned you against Colonel Tintin . . . Look at this letter and tell me if I was wrong . . .

REPUBLIC OF NUEVO-RICO
★★★
WAR OFFICE   SECRET

Dear Colonel Tintin,
We have safely received the plans of the 75 TRGP which the government of San Theodoros has just acquired.
As promised, the agreed fee will now be paid to you.
X.14

A spy! . . . ¡Mil bombas! Planted as a spy! . . . The traitor! . . . The rat! . . . He'll pay dearly for this!

Hello! . . . Hello! . . . Colonel Juanitos? . . . Take ten men and go and arrest Colonel Tintin at once! . . . Eh? What? . . . That's an order, Colonel! . . . Move!

Meanwhile . . .

The explosion is set for 11 a.m. . . . What's the time? . . . Hello, my watch has stopped!

Now, let's put it right . . .

CALLE DEL SOL

Come in!

RAT TAT TAT

Good morning, Colonel Juanitos. Good to see you . . .

I'm terribly sorry, Colonel Tintin, but I've been ordered to arrest you!

Arrest me? . . . Me?? . . .

There's been a power cut this morning, so all the municipal clocks have stopped. Go and put them right.

Ten o'clock. There's still some time before I need to deposit my little box of fireworks!

Ah, General Alcazar, you're going to repent making me a corporal! Insult me at your peril! Corporal Diaz takes his revenge!

Yes, you can take these: they're my orders. The first concerns Colonel Tintin: he will be shot at dawn tomorrow. The other is for Corporal Diaz, my former aide-de-camp. I've made him a colonel again. He can resume his duties at once.

Back in gaol again! Unless I'm much mistaken, my friend Trickler has cooked this one up to get rid of me.

Oh! . . . It won't be easy to escape . . .

Nightfall, and I still can't see any way out . . . There must be something . . .

Pull up the string: a rope is attached to it. Tie the rope firmly to the bars. When you're ready, wave your handkerchief. As soon as the bars have gone, jump out of the window.

Ah, here comes the rope . . .

That's it: he's signalling! Pull!

!

Hello?

Come on, jump! Quick!

Follow me! Hurry! They've raised the alarm.

Pablo, I'll never forget what you've done for me!

Come . . . Quickly!

Take no notice! They shoot like a bunch of drunks!

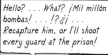

There. Take the car and go. By midday tomorrow you'll be over the frontier. Don't worry about me: I've covered my tracks. I shan't have any trouble. Goodbye, señor Tintin.

Goodbye, dear Pablo. I shall remember . . .

It is nothing, señor. I haven't forgotten that day you spared my life!

Hello? . . . What? ¡Mil millón bombas! . . . !?¿¡ . . . Recapture him, or I'll shoot every guard at the prison!

I can't just run them over . . . I'll stop, and play it carefully . . .

Perfect! They've moved out of the way! On we go!

?!?

Caramba! It was him!

Tintin went past in a car . . . heading south!

I want him, dead or alive!

There!!

It's him! . . . Open fire!

RAT TAT TAT TAT

Snakes! I'm being followed!

CRACK

?

TOOOOOOT

Caramba! A train!! . . . We've got him. The road crosses the railway. He'll have to stop, or he'll be smashed to smithereens!

Tintin, my friend, this time it's all or nothing . . .

38

He's going . . . !!

The fool!

Whew!

We cut things a bit fine there . . . eh, Snowy?

Now, step on the gas! We'll get him in the mountains.

Mountains! That's bad. Their car's much more powerful, and they'll soon catch us up . . .

Tintin! You'll kill us!

He went over . . .

Caramba! What a drop!

I'm staying here. Why climb down? He's had it anyway, hasn't he?

As you like. I'm going to see . . .

There it is. We can go back to Las Dopicos. That's put paid to Colonel Tintin.

VRROOM
What's going on up there?
That's our car!
?

!

He . . . he must have been hiding behind the rocks. I didn't see him coming . . .

It doesn't matter. He'll be caught at the frontier. It can't be far from here. We'll pick him up there. Come on!

?
It's a government car!

If they stop me, I'm caught . . . and if that's a strong barrier, I'm dead.

PAAAARP

CRACK

!

Hello? . . . Border post 31? . . . Patrol No. 4 here . . . A San-Theodorian car with a mounted machine-gun just raced past here, heading for the frontier.

Red alert! . . . San-Theodorian armoured car reported . . . Man your posts!

?

RATATATAT

Watch out, Snowy! . . . They're shooting at our tyres!

An armoured car tried to attack border post 31. It was destroyed and one of the occupants, a colonel, was taken prisoner.

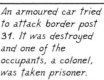

General! . . . General! . . . This dispatch has just come by telephone!

"An armoured car . . ." !!! This time it's war! That's what they want: that's what they'll get!

Pass this communiqué to the newspapers. I want special editions on the streets in an hour!

Sanfacion Star! . . . Extra! . . . Extra! . . . Sanfacion Star! . . . Extra!

WAR! IT'S WAR! A motorised column of the San-Theodorian army mounted a surprise attack today, but the enemy were repulsed by our valiant troops, who inflicted heavy casualties . . .

Hello? . . . Mr Trickler? . . . Success! The Nuevo-Ricans have just declared war on us! . . . Yes . . . over some new incident on the border . . .

The Gran Chapo fields are ours! . . . Once again General American Oil has beaten British South-American Petrol!

In a fortnight all the Gran Chapo will be in Nuevo-Rican hands. Then I hope you in British South-American Petrol will not forget your promises.

The first chance we get, we desert, and . . .

. . . we look for thees fetish again.

(42)

Meanwhile . . .
What will happen to me?

I don't know. We've been ordered to take you to Sanfacion, and that's all.

Good old Snowy! . . . Keep on chewing!

Free!

SANFACION

This is it! Out we go!

BANG BANG

BANG BANG

BANG

WOOAAAH!

SPLOSH

43

If I can't reach that rock. I'm done for!

Whew!

WOOAH!

Well, what do we do now?

?

A tree trunk! . . . Don't let it go . . . it could be our only chance!

Ah! It's swinging round!

That's it . . .
We can get across
. . . with luck!

We're safe now, Snowy.

The first thing is to find out where we are . . .

Meanwhile . . .

Caramba! Listen to this, Ramón . . .

Drama at sea. The liner "Ville de Lyon" caught fire last night in mid-ocean. Agency reports state that passengers and crew are safe, but all cargo and baggage have been destroyed.

The fetish! The fetish burnt!

Unless . . . unless thees Tintin is lying when he tell us thees fetish is in hees trunk . . .

A house, at long last!

He's lost, and is seeking shelter? . . . But of course, bring him in . . .

Don José Trujillo owns this hacienda . . . He is very happy to welcome you.

That evening . . .

So the river is the Coliflor? . . . Don't the Arumbayas live somewhere along the banks of the Coliflor?

Yes, they do. But there aren't many who'd dare go that way. The Arumbayas are the fiercest Indians in the whole of South America. The last man to try was a British explorer, Ridgewell. He went more than ten years ago. He's never been seen since.

Oh!

D'you think there's anyone who'd agree to take me there?

?

Next morning . . .

This is Caraco, an Indian who knows the river well. But I doubt if he'd dare go . . . there.

I want to go down-river. Will you act as my guide?

Si, señor.

I . . . er . . . I want to visit the Arumbayas . . .

!

Arumbayas! Very bad people! No! Caraco no go!

Chicken!

Wait, Caraco. Think it over. Look what I'll pay you . . .

Caraco go. But Caraco very poor man. The señor will buy canoe of Caraco.

All right, I'll buy it.

Caraco know other white señor. He want to go to Arumbayas. Long, long time ago. Other white señor . . .

I know, he never came back . . .

And that doesn't bother you?

Several days later . . .

Soon is night, señor.

You're right. We must stop.

Tomorrow, we come to country of Arumbayas.

Goodnight, señor . . .

Goodnight, Caraco.

Next morning . . .

Where's Caraco?

The canoe is still there, anyway . . .

CARACO!

He's left me! . . . Now I understand why he wanted me to buy his canoe . . . So I could go on alone!

Careful now! . . . Rapids!

The canoe! . . . The canoe, with the guns and the food! . . . All gone!

Well! Now I really am in a jam! . . . No gun, no food, in hostile country . . . and all by myself!

!?! . . . I don't count any more, I suppose?

It's funny, but I have a feeling somebody's watching us . . .

Y . . . y . . . you . . . th-th-think . . . s-so?

OH!

A dart! . . . It's sure to be poisoned! . . . D'you remember, Snowy? . . . Curare!

? ! ?

I can't hear anything now. I must have shaken them off . . .

?

Cowards! Come on out and show yourselves, unless you're afraid to!

Tintin, you'll get yourself killed!

WOOAH!

!

Great snakes!

A white man!

Who are you? And what brings you to this place?

My name is Tintin . . . who . . . who are you?

My name is Ridgewell.

Ridgewell? The explorer? But everybody thinks you're dead.

What a pity! Or rather, what a good thing, because I've decided never to return to civilisation. I'm happy here among the Arumbayas, whose life I share . . .

And whose weapons you've adopted. What was the meaning of that little game of darts?

I just wanted you to have an unfriendly reception, to encourage you to leave at once. Believe me, if I'd wanted to kill you it wouldn't have taken more than one dart. Look, I'll prove it. You see that big flower over there?

Yes.

Good shot!

? WOOAAAAH!

Ooh! I'm so sorry!

WOOAAAH!

Don't worry, the dart wasn't poisoned. Use my handkerchief for a bandage.

Now, tell me how you come to be here in this country . . .

Well, it's like this. An Arumbaya fetish in a museum in Europe, brought back by the explorer Walker, was stolen and replaced by a copy. I noticed the substitution. Two other men were also on the track of the real fetish and whoever had stolen it.

I followed these two men to South America. They killed the thief on board ship and stole his fetish. But this one too was a fake. So now I'm trying to find the real fetish, and I still don't know where it is.

. . . Just as I still don't know what they were all after: Tortilla, the first thief, and his two killers. They all wanted the fetish. But why they wanted it is still a complete mystery. So I thought perhaps that here . . .

. . . among the Arumbayas I might learn something fresh about it . . .

Perhaps you may. It's quite possible . . .

Rumbabas! . . . Sworn enemies of the Arumbayas! . . .

What will they do to us? That's easy! They'll cut off our heads and by a most ingenious process they'll shrink them to the size of an apple!

Ahw wada lu'vali bahn chaco conats! Ha! ha! ha!

Just as I thought. He means our heads will soon be added to his collection!

They've gone . . . Snowy, you've absolutely got to save Tintin.

If I can find the Arumbaya village, and take this thing to them, perhaps they'll understand that its owner is in danger . . .

Meanwhile, in the Arumbaya village . . .

The Spirits tell me that if your son is to be cured, he must eat the heart of the first animal you meet in the forest . . .

I go, most powerful one!

What a strange animal! . . . And what's it carrying in its mouth? A quiver! That's funny . . . I must try to catch it alive . . .

See, O witch-doctor. This cloth belongs to the old bearded one, and the quiver also. Perhaps the old bearded one is in danger?

You mind your own business! . . . Give me the animal and go! . . . I shall kill the creature and take out its heart; this I shall give to your son to eat. Go now!

And if you breathe one word of all this, I shall call down the Spirits upon you and your family . . . and you will all be changed into frogs!

No danger now: he won't gossip . . . But he's right. The old bearded one may be in trouble. All the better! Let's hope he dies! Then I shall regain my power over the Arumbayas. Now, before I kill the animal I must burn these things . . . they might give me away.

Great Spirits of the forest, we bring thee a sacrifice of these two strangers . . .

Stop, O chief of the Rumbabas! The Spirits of the forest do not accept your sacrifice!

These two strangers are friends of the forest. You will set them free.

V-v-very w-w-. . . well!

It's magic . . . witchcraft!

Magic? . . . Didn't you realise it was me speaking? . . . I'm a ventriloquist . . . Ventriloquism, I'd have you know my young friend, is my pet hobby.

Good heavens!

Brother Arumbayas, you are about to witness a remarkable phenomenon . . .

My end!

We will take out this animal's heart and give it, still beating, to our sick brother . . .

YAAH!

The old bearded one!

The villain! . . . Lucky you decided to come and look for us Karamelo . . . otherwise we'd have been too late.

Let me introduce Avakuki, chief of the Arumbayas.

Owar ya? Ts goota meecha mai 'tee.

It's a pleasure, sir . . .

Naluk, Djarem membah dabrah nai dul? Tintin zluk infu rit'h. Kanyah elpim?

Dabrah nai dul? Oi, oi! Slaika toljah. Datrai b'giv dabrah nai dul ta'Walker. Ewuz anais-gi. Buttiz'h felaz tukahr presh usdjel. Enefda Arumbayas ket chimdai lavis gutsfa gahtah'z. Nomess in'h!

I was just asking the chief about the fetish, and this is what he told me . . . You'll be interested . . .

I'm all ears!

? ?

Nitwits!

Cohrluv ahduk! Ai tolja tahitta ferlip inbaul intada oh'l! Andatdohn meenis ferlip ineer oh'l!

I should never have started to teach them golf! They just can't learn to play properly!

!

But to come back to the fetish. The elders of the tribe still remember about the Walker expedition. It's quite a tale. They know that a fetish was offered as a token of friendship to Walker during his stay with the tribe. But as soon as the explorers had left . . .

the Arumbayas discovered that a sacred stone had disappeared. It seems that the stone gave protection from snake-bite to anyone who touched it. The tribe remembered a half-caste named Lopez, the explorers' interpreter, who was often seen prowling around the hut where the magic stone was kept under guard.

The Arumbayas were furious. They set off in pursuit of the expedition, caught up with them, and massacred almost all the party . . . Walker himself managed to escape, carrying the fetish. As for the half-caste, although badly wounded, he too got away. The stone, probably a diamond, was never recovered . . . That's how the story goes.

Now I understand . . . The whole thing makes sense!

Listen! . . . The half-caste steals the stone, and to avoid suspicion he conceals it in the fetish. He thinks he'll be able to get it back later on . . .

But the Arumbayas attack the expedition and Lopez is wounded. He has to flee without the diamond. And that's it! . . . The diamond is still in its hiding-place, and that's why Tortilla, and after him his two killers, tried to steal the fetish.

It looks to me as if you're right!

So now all I have to do is find the fetish . . . and return to Europe!

Some days later . . .

Meanwhile . . .

REPUBLIC OF SAN THEODOROS
NOTICE

DESERTERS
ALONSO PERF?
RAMON BADA

We simply must get hold of a canoe . . .

Look! . . . There ees canoe . . . and weeth one man only . . . But . . . I theenk I am seeing theengs . . . or ees a dream . . . Thees man . . .

Caramba! . . . It's Tintin!

We'll rest here for a while before we continue our journey . . .

So we meet again, eh?

?

Let's start talking! . . . Did you know the 'Ville de Lyon' had been completely destroyed by fire . . . burnt out!

Really?

Yes, really! And the fetish you left in your trunk has been destroyed! . . . Burnt! . . . All because of you . . . You are going to pay dearly, my friend!

No! I told you . . . The real fetish wasn't aboard . . .

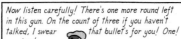

Oho! So you lied to us! Well, now you're going to tell us where it is. And don't try to fool us again!

I've already told you: I know nothing about it . . .

Now listen carefully! There's one more round left in this gun. On the count of three if you haven't talked, I swear that bullet's for you! One! . . . two! . . .

Look out! A snake!!! . . .

Where?

YOW!

Here!

OOH!

Caramba!!!

!?

Ha! ha! ha! I've got you at last! . . .

Good! . . . Now they're safely taken care of, let's see what he's got in his wallet.

OHO!

Arambaya. I am dying Valker expedition the diamond in the fetish the broken ear
Lopez

Where did you get this note? . . . Tell me!

In the ship, on our way to Europe. Tortilla dropped it. But we didn't know what it meant. Tortilla was just a fellow passenger. We only realised the significance of the paper when we read about the fetish being stolen from the museum . . . Then we decided we'd try to get the fetish away from Tortilla.

Excellent! . . . Now, the only thing we don't know is how Tortilla got hold of this note. But since he's dead, I don't suppose we'll ever discover that! . . . So now, gentlemen, let's get moving!

And behave yourselves!

What are you planning to do with us?

No problem. I shall hand you over to justice. I think you well deserve it!

Hand us over to justice? . . .
Ha! ha! ha!
!

Don't count your chickens before they're hatched, my fine friend . . .
Teep heem een! . . .
?

Got you!
Bravo!

There! . . .
Hee's feenished! Look, Alonso. Thees piranhas, thees man-eating feeshes . . . they come for heem already.

Caramba! I didn't hit him hard enough. Look! He's recovered . . . He's reached the bank . . .

Bah! Leave heem! We shall be in Sanfacion long before heem . . .

No point in trying to recapture them for the moment . . .

We've got a tough job, Snowy old boy. We've got to make the journey on foot.

Off we go!

Several days later . . .

Sanfacion at last! . . . Thank goodness! . . . I really thought we'd never make it! . . .

To Europe? . . . A boat left yesterday. Now I'm afraid you'll have to wait for a week.

A whole week! Oh well, we'll use the time to get rested and sort ourselves out . . .

Listen to this, Snowy! . . . "The geological survey party just returned from the Gran Chapo report that they found no trace of oil in the area."

A week later . . .

. . . the news . . . A ceasefire has been arranged between the forces of San Theodoros and Nuevo-Rico. It is believed that a peace treaty will be signed in the near future.

Home again! It's good to be back where we belong, isn't it Snowy? . . . All we need now is to unearth the fetish, and everything in the garden will be lovely!

Good heavens! ... It's fantastic!

Think of the thousands of miles I've travelled to find this thing!

£100 ... Cheap at the price! ... But come to think of it, I should have asked how he managed to get hold of the fetish ...

?!?

£17.50 THE PAIR

!?! ... There's no mistake ... They've both got a broken ear! ... I can't believe it ... It's absolutely incredible!

This time I really will find out where they came from!

Good morning. Would you be kind enough to tell me who brought you those two fetishes?

Ah, yes, the two little fetishes ... who brought them to me? ...

A bit of a struggle, but at last I've got the address ... Mr Balthazar, 32 Lamb's Lane ... That isn't very far. We'll go straight there.

J. BALTHAZAR

32

This is it.

OFFICES AND WORKSHOPS

Here we are ...

OFFICES AND WORKSHOPS

Are you Mr Balthazar . . . brother of the sculptor who . . . er? . . .

Yes, I am. What do you want?

I wondered if you could perhaps tell me how you found the fetish you used as a model . . .

Oh, that's easy enough. I was rummaging around my late brother's things. The fetish was at the bottom of a trunk . . . But why do you ask?

Er . . . it's a long story . . . But . . . you've still got the original?

It's a funny thing . . . someone else came to ask me exactly that question, only three days ago . . . No, I haven't got it. I sold it. But I can tell you the address of the man who bought it.

Mr Samuel Goldbarr . . . a rich American! Snowy, we're going to pull it off . . . We'll find the real fetish!

I'd like to speak to Mr Goldbarr.

Mr Goldbarr is not at home, sir.

But, sir, I cannot . . .

That's all right. I'll wait for him.

But sir, you'll have a long wait.

It doesn't matter. I've got plenty of time.

But sir, Mr Goldbarr has left for America . . .

Left for America!!! . . . Oh!!

. . . He's sailing today aboard the SS Washington. Perhaps, if you hurry . . .

. . . and of course he had to take the fetish with him! That's just my luck!

Ex . . . ex . . . excuse me . . . the . . . the . . . the SS WASH . . . WASHINGTON?

That's her out there. If you wanted to board her you're too late. She sailed an hour ago.

But if you really want to catch her, maybe you could hitch a ride from the air-base over there . . . It's not far . . .

NO EN
EXCEP

. . . catch the "Washington", eh? . . . Hmm . . . maybe . . . We happen to have a plane going out to her . . . to deliver some mail . . .

First service for lunch, please! . . . First service for lunch! . . .

F·MAB

F·MAB

There goes Goldbarr . . . He's off to lunch. Now's our chance!

82

Ramón! . . . Ramón! . . . Look! . . . I've got it!

59

Here comes the mail . . .

But the diamond . . . Where is it?

Eet must be somewhere inside . . .

Leesten, Alonso . . . We cannot stay here any longer. Ees too reesky. Someone might come. We take thees fetish to our cabin then we take our time to look . . .

Hello . . . there's a passenger . . .

I need to speak to one of your passengers immediately . . . A Mr Goldbarr . . .

Mr Goldbarr? You'll find him in the first-class dining-room.

Let's hope I've come in time!

! ? TINTIN!

Hands up! . . .

OH!

The diamond!

Look out! Thees diamond!

It'll go into the sea!

Ees lost! . . . Ees because of you . . . You pay for thees!

AAH! ✱ WOOAH BANG BANG ✱ HELP! ✱

Three men overboard, Sir! . . .

?!

Someone said there were three of them . . .

Look! . . . They're fishing one out now . . .

The . . . the others? . . .

. . . Went straight on down!

61

Oooh! My fetish! My beautiful fetish!

Mr Goldbarr? . . . I'm terribly sorry your fetish has been damaged. I can explain everything if you'll allow me . . .

. . . I think you should know that your fetish is stolen property.

Stolen?! . . . But I . . .

Yes, I know where you bought it, and I'm sure the man who sold it to you acted in good faith . . .

If that's the case, I wouldn't consider keeping the fetish for a moment longer. If you're going back on shore, can I ask you to take it and restore it to the museum where it belongs? I'd be greatly obliged!

OF ETHNOGR

May I please speak to the Director?

And now, Snowy my friend, we're going to take a well-earned rest!

Wooah! Wooah!

Toreador, ♪♩ on guard now! Torea-♫ Toreador! dor!

ARUMBAYA FETISH
The Arumbaya tribe live along the banks of the River Coliflor in the Republic of South America

THE REAL-LIFE INSPIRATION BEHIND TINTIN'S ADVENTURES

Written by Stuart Tett
with the collaboration of Studio Moulinsart.

Discover something new and exciting

HERGÉ

The Hergé Museum

PAINTED POSTS DAHOMEY

Hergé loved to visit museums. On the first page of this story he drew himself looking around the Museum of Ethnography. The photo below shows the Hergé Museum in Belgium, which opened on May 22 (Hergé's birthday), 2009. Want to dive into the universe created by Hergé? Come and visit!

© Moulinsart–Architect: Christian de Portzamparc

about Tintin and his creator Hergé!

TINTIN

At home

We don't often get to see Tintin in his apartment at 26 Labrador Road: in later adventures Tintin moves in with his friend Captain Haddock. On page 1 of *The Broken Ear*, we catch a rare glimpse of the brave reporter doing his morning exercises. Even Snowy gives it a try!

THE TRUE STORY
…behind *The Broken Ear*

The story of *The Broken Ear* begins and ends in the Museum of Ethnography. Hergé sometimes drew inspiration from real museums, and in the 1930s he visited the Cinquantenaire Museums in Brussels.

Once upon a time…

In 1880, to celebrate the fiftieth anniversary of the independence of Belgium, an old military training ground just east of Brussels was annexed to the city and turned into a beautiful park: the Cinquantenaire (meaning "fiftieth anniversary") Park. Today there are several museums at this location. For this story, Hergé was inspired by objects from the Non-European civilizations collection in the Royal Museum of Art and History.

The Royal Museum of Art and History, the Cinquantenaire Museums

Tintin's Imaginary Museum

In 1979 an exhibition celebrating 50 years of Tintin was organized at the Centre for Fine Arts in Brussels. Hergé drew the catalogue cover for the exhibition, which you can see on the right. ▶

A few days after the photo below (showing Hergé at the exhibition) was taken, someone stole the master copy of the statue with the broken ear, just like in the story! Hergé was astonished to receive an anonymous note saying that if he came to the exhibition at

a certain time with a copy of *The Broken Ear* under his left arm, the statue would be returned. The playful author showed up with the book under his *right* arm. There was no sign of the thief or the statue. Although certain people would later claim to have perpetrated the copycat crime, it has never been fully solved. Truth is stranger than fiction!

▼

Off to South America

In the story, when the tribal statue is stolen from the Museum of Ethnography and then apparently returned, Tintin is quick to realize that the case is still open. Events lead the reporter to San Theodoros in South America, where he is involuntarily conscripted into the army as personal assistant to General Alcazar. Enter Mr R.W. Trickler from General American Oil, who will stop at nothing to get rich.

> *Of course, of course. But you could render us invaluable service. I mentioned that part of the oil fields lie in Nuevo-Rican territory. My company wishes to exploit the whole region: so it follows that you must take over the area.*
>
> *But . . . that would mean war!*

Once upon a time...

Hergé based the countries of San Theodoros and its neighbor Nuevo-Rico on Bolivia and Paraguay. In 1928, a few years before the author began writing *The Broken Ear*, oil was discovered on the edge of some disputed territory—the Gran Chaco region—that lay between the two countries.

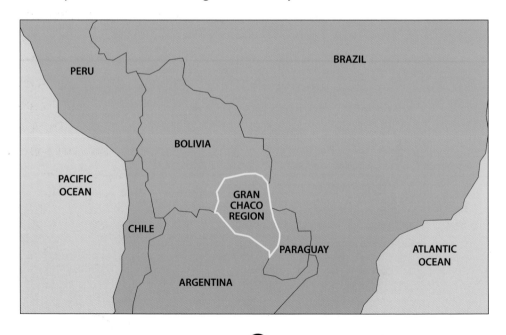

The Gran Chaco War

Although Bolivia claimed the legal rights to the Gran Chaco, in reality Paraguayans had settled much of the habitable land. Due to the arid nature of the land, the dispute had never gotten out of hand, but the prospect of hidden oil reserves changed everything. Full-scale war between Bolivia and its neighbour Paraguay broke out in 1932.

Look, General . . . just think . . . It's wholly to your advantage. As I say, you declare war on Neuvo-Rico, and you annexe the oilfields. My company makes a profit on the oil and your country gets 35%. But naturally you deduct 10% for personal expenses . . .

It's clear in the frame above that somebody knows how to sweet-talk General Alcazar! Mr Trickler's rival from British South-American Petrol is surely having the same conversation with the leader of Nuevo-Rico. In the real-life war, which ended in 1935 with Paraguay winning most of the disputed territory, Standard Oil supported Bolivia and Shell Oil backed Paraguay. But it was all for nothing: no more oil was discovered in the region.

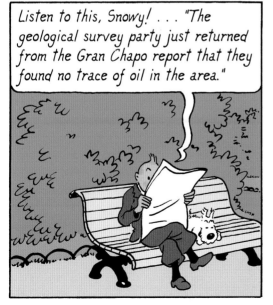

Listen to this, Snowy! . . . "The geological survey party just returned from the Gran Chapo report that they found no trace of oil in the area."

It's amazing to see how Hergé incorporated historical events into his stories. But in this case there is one small difference between the story and reality: Hergé changed the name of the region from Gran Chaco to Gran Chapo, which means "big hat" in French—a pun on the sombrero (a large South American hat)!

No escape!

Tintin has been cornered by fearsome Rumbaba warriors, but before he even got to the jungle he was outnumbered. Framed as a spy by Trickler and Bazarov, Tintin had been jailed but then managed to escape. He had been hoping to find out more about the mysterious statue by meeting the jungle tribes, but he hadn't been counting on such a frosty reception!

Hergé based his South American tribes—both the Arumbayas and the Rumbabas—on the real-life Jivaros. The Jivaro tribe comes from the eastern slopes of the Andes mountains, in Ecuador and Peru.

Once upon a time...

For hundreds of years the Jivaro peoples were renowned as fierce warriors, successfully fighting off attacks by the Incas and the Spanish in the fifteenth and sixteenth centuries. Both the use of the blowpipe weapon and the custom of shrinking heads are Jivaro traditions.

Over the last century, demand by tourists generated a trade in shrunken heads; at the time this story was written, in the 1930s, you could buy a shrunken head for around £15 (£250 today)!

Now let's **Explore and Discover!**

EXPLORE AND DISCOVER

Looking through the first couple of pages of this story is like walking around a real museum. Let's take a little tour of the exhibits!

PAINTED POSTS DAHOMEY

Polychrome Dahomey posts,
Trocadero Ethnographic Museum, Paris
(photo: Hergé's archives)

No. 3542

Pre-Columbian wooden statue from the Royal Museum of Art and History, Brussels

Baule tribal masks
(photo: Hergé's archives)

BAPENDE MASK
15

Pende mask from the Royal Museum for Central Africa, Turvuren, Brussels (photo: Hergé's archives)

Hergé copied real objects from the Royal Museum of Art and History in the Cinquantenaire Park, the Trocadero Museum in Paris and the Royal Museum for Central Africa on the outskirts of Brussels, Belgium.

Senufo "firespitter" mask from the Ivory Coast

HEAD OF CARVED WOOD PACHACAMAO
1783

OLD AGE ADVERSARY

It looks like Tintin has discovered a sinister link between the stolen statue and the death of sculptor Mr Balthazar—someone has just tried to run him down! Luckily a passerby caught the vehicle's registration number, but when Tintin investigates he is surprised to find out that his would-be attacker is apparently an old man...with an equally antiquated car and chauffeur!

Hergé faithfully copied a Hotchkiss type V automobile, which was made around 1910. The model in this photo may have been an old car by the time Hergé wrote *The Broken Ear*, but it was still going strong— apparently it had clocked up over 200,000 miles and was still running!

EXOTIC BIRDS

★ The cheeky green parrot plays a key role in the story, and at one point he escapes into the sky above Brussels, Belgium.

★ In 1974, nearly 40 years after Hergé began writing *The Broken Ear*, about 40 green parakeets (small parrots) were let loose from an aviary in Brussels.

★ Today, nearly another 40 years later, there are over 10,000 of these birds living in the parks of Brussels. Look at the Belgian bird on this page!

★ Hergé tried hard to add real-life details to The Adventures of Tintin; sometimes it seems like real life was inspired by Hergé's stories!

A REAL AEROPLANE

After days of squawking insults and biting people's fingers, the green parrot finally tells the gangsters what they want to know. They catch a flight to the French port of Le Havre. Hergé copied a real aeroplane: the Wibault-Penhoët 283-T-12. Check out the photo below!

EL LIBERTADOR

In South America, Tintin plays chess with General Alcazar while Corporal Diaz hides behind a statue of General Olivaro, the liberator of San Theodoros. Hergé was inspired by a real historical character when he created this statue.

SIMON BOLIVAR—EL LIBERTADOR

★ Simon Bolivar was born in Caracas, the capital city of Venezuela, in 1783. Although his parents died before he was 10 years old, Simon Bolivar received a good education and was trained at a military academy from the age of 14.

★ Deeply impressed by the spirit of revolution he came across during his European travels, Simon Bolivar took an oath in 1805 to free South America from Spanish control.

★ Beginning with the conquest of his native country of Venezuela in 1813, Simon Bolivar also brought revolution to Colombia, Panama, Ecuador, Peru and Upper Peru, which became known as Bolivia in his honor.

★ The photo on the left shows a statue of Simon Bolivar, created in 1959 by the American sculptor Felix Weihs de Weldon. It stands in Washington, D.C.

SIMON BOLIVAR
THE LIBERATOR

BORN JULY 24 1783
CARACAS VENEZUELA
DIED DECEMBER 17 1830
SANTA MARTA COLOMBIA

AL
GENERAL
OLIVARO
LIBERTADOR
DE
SAN TEODORO

BANANAS

Assassination attempts follow in quick succession in San Theodoros. After several narrow escapes, Tintin is saved by a bunch of bananas! Even though he was very careful, Hergé sometimes made mistakes. He drew the bananas growing downward, when in reality they grow up. This mistake can be traced to a photo in his archives (shown on the right), showing a bunch of bananas upside down.

The right way up!

BASIL BAZAROV

Any hope that Tintin might have of talking General Alcazar out of war is crushed by the arrival of the unscrupulous arms dealer Basil Bazarov. Hergé openly based this character on the real-life Sir Basil Zaharoff (1849–1936).

★ After starting life as a petty criminal and smuggler, Basil Zaharoff began a career as a weapons salesman when he was 28 years old.

★ Zaharoff sold a faulty submarine to Greece and then convinced Turkey that its neighbour was a threat! One of the two submarines he sold Turkey overbalanced when test-firing a torpedo and dove vertically into the sea.

★ The cunning arms trader bought a newspaper to ensure favorable press, and a bank to assist with financing.

★ By the end of his life, Zaharoff had become extraordinarily rich and powerful. He was even knighted in Great Britain!

Nordenfelt II submarine sold to Turkey by Basil Zaharoff (1886)

GENERAL ALCAZAR

General Alcazar spends half his time as a revolutionary and the other half as a dictator. Hergé read about real-life Latin American dictators, such as Alfredo Stroessner of Paraguay.

★ Alfredo Stroessner ruled Paraguay from 1954 to 1989. He was deposed by a coup and lived in Brazil until his death in 2006 at the age of 93.

★ Augusto Pinochet was the president of Chile from 1974 to 1990. His time in office was marked by the brutal suppression of opposition. Pinochet was arrested in the UK and Chile at the end of his life but was never convicted of any of the numerous crimes he was accused of committing.

★ In 1972, Guillermo Rodríguez Lara, also known as "Bombita", took control of Ecuador by a coup. Although he used money made from oil reserves to build hospitals, schools and roads, Bombita was deposed in 1976.

You wouldn't want to get on the wrong side of General Alcazar, or you could be facing a firing squad! Yet, despite his tough approach, the general can't seem to hold on to power. When we meet him in Tintin's final complete adventure, *Tintin and the Picaros*, he has been ousted by his rival and is trying to start a new revolution. Not another one!

RIDGEWELL

British explorer Ridgewell decided to leave "civilization" behind and has been living with the Arumbaya tribe in the jungle along the banks of the River Coliflor for over ten years! Hergé had heard about the real-life adventures of British explorer Percy Fawcett (pictured far right) and based this character on him.

★ In 1906, British army officer Colonel Percy Fawcett (1867–unknown) accepted a job offer from the Royal Geographic Society to travel to South America to map unknown territories.

★ Fawcett believed in treating the indigenous peoples with kindness. His men once charmed an aggressive tribe by playing music and singing.

★ Fawcett encountered many dangerous animals on his explorations. Once he shot a 62-foot anaconda. A fellow adventurer had two fingers bitten off by piranhas while washing his hands in a river.

★ Fawcett became convinced that there was an ancient city—he called it "Z"— hidden in the Brazilian jungle. In 1925 he set off with his son Jack to find it. They were never seen again.

★ Some people think that Fawcett was killed by wild animals. Others think that he became a tribal chief and lived the rest of his life in the jungle!

EXOTIC LANGUAGES

Hergé came up with an ingenious language for his fictional native peoples to speak. He used words from a particular Brussels dialect—Brusseleir—that his grandmother spoke, adding and removing spaces between letters to make it look like an exotic language. When the Tintin books were published in English, the translators gave the natives some British slang vocabulary and strong London accents, but also mixed up letters and used phonetics—spelling words like they sound—to make the words look foreign. Look at the panels here and check out the "translations".

Naluk, Djarem membah dabrah nai dul? Tintin zluk infu rit'h. Kanyah elpim?

Dabrah nai dul? Oi, oi! Slaika toljah. Datrai b'giv dabrah nai dul ta'Walker. Ewuz anais-gi. Buttiz'h felaz tukahr presh usdjel. Enefda Arumbayas ket chimdai lavis gutsfa gahtah'z. Nomess in'h!

Ridgewell: "Now look. Do you remember the brown idol [statue]? Tintin's looking for it. Can you help him?"

Chief: "The brown idol? Listen! It's like I told you. The tribe gave the brown idol to Walker. He was a nice guy. But his fellows took our precious jewel. And after the Arumbayas catch him, I'll have his guts for garters [I'll teach him a lesson], no messing!"

Cohrluv ahduk! Ai tolja tahitta ferlip inbaul intada oh'l! Andatdohn meenis ferlip ineer oh'l!

"Cor love a duck! I told you to hit the flipping ball into the hole. And that doesn't mean his flipping ear hole!"

What is the Jivaro saying in the panel on the right? Try to work it out yourself!

Brusseleir

Look at the original French picture next to the English.
Hergé's Brussels dialect (highlighted) means something different!

Chief: "How are you? It's good to meet you, matey [friend]."

Ridgewell: "Let me introduce 'Bald Grandma,' chief of the Arumbayas."

Chief: "It's 'Grandpa': I'm not some stupid old woman…What nonsense!"

BACK TO BELGIUM

Tintin finally manages to escape the villains, the piranhas and even the flying golf balls—soon he is back in Belgium and his adventure is nearly over. Tintin is astonished to come across a workshop full of statues. Today, if you go to the museum shop at the Royal Museum of Art and History in Brussels, you can see that someone has had the same idea! Look at the photo below. ▼

The museum shop, The Royal Museum of Art and History, Brussels, Belgium, 2011

TINTIN'S GRAND ADVENTURE

The Broken Ear is an appealing story for different reasons. Younger readers find the action and adventure exciting, while the political humour makes grown-ups laugh. It's also a clever detective story. Now Hergé was learning to create multi-faceted stories that fans of all ages could enjoy, a bit like *The Simpsons* today!

Trivia: *The Broken Ear*

When, in 1942, Hergé began the task of reformatting and colouring the black-and-white Tintin stories, he started with The Broken Ear. The drawings in the colour version you have just read are simply the original black-and-white drawings coloured in.

Some Tintin experts think that the bearded man walking into the museum in the first frame of page 1 is the same man who claims to be the Consul for Poldavia in The Blue Lotus (pp.54-55). Is this dubious diplomat in fact the thief Tortilla?

Colonel Percy Fawcett may have inspired filmmakers George Lucas and Steven Spielberg (creator of the 2011 Tintin movie) when they dreamed up the character of Indiana Jones.

Look at the last page of your Young Readers Edition of The Blue Lotus: the original front cover of this story shows Tintin hiding in a vase. Look at the second to last frame on page 1 of The Broken Ear: Tintin brought the vase back to Belgium!

les aventures de
TINTIN
reporter

L'OREILLE CASSÉE

CASTERMAN

The original cover for *The Broken Ear* (1937)